£2.00

3/24

40

UNUSUAL PIZZA RECIPES
FROM AROUND THE WORLD

Table of Contents

1. BEET PESTO PIZZA WITH KALE & GOAT CHEESE

INGREDIENTS

- 1 lb. gluten-free pizza dough
- 1 cup beet pesto
- 2 cups kale leaves thinly sliced*
- 1 1/2 cups of mozzarella cheese grated
- 2 ounces goat cheese

*I used lacinato (dino) kale

INSTRUCTIONS

Prepare the beet pesto and the pizza dough.

Preheat the oven to 415 degrees F.

Dust gluten-free flour (or cornmeal) on a baking sheet and press or roll the dough to desired thickness.

Bake the dough for 5 to 7 minutes with no toppings.

Remove the crust from the oven and spread the beet pesto over it. Add the kale leaves, followed by the goat cheese and mozzarella. Note: the kale will cook down in the oven.

Bake pizza for 20 to 25 minutes or to desired crisp.

Allow pizza to cool 5 minutes before serving.

2. CARAMELIZED ONIONS, APPLES & GOAT CHEESE PIZZA

INGREDIENTS

- 1 large onion, sliced thinly
- 1 apple cored and sliced thinly
- 4 ounces herbed goat cheese at room temperature
- 3 sprigs thyme
- 2 tablespoons honey (for drizzling)
- 4 tablespoons regular butter (or vegan)

INSTRUCTIONS

Preheat your oven to 375 degrees F.

In a pan over medium heat, melt two tablespoons of the butter. When pan is hot, add the onions and swirl around so they are covered, and cook down for fifteen minutes until soft, swirling every five minutes so they don't burn.

While these are cooking, heat the remaining two (2) tablespoons in pan over medium high heat and add the apple slices and cook down for ten minutes until soft. Remove from heat when finished.

Spread the goat cheese over the pizza crust. Add the apples, then the onions on top.

Bake for ten (10) minutes in the oven until the goat cheese is slightly melted.

3. STRAWBERRY BALSAMIC PIZZA WITH CHICKEN, SWEET ONION & APPLEWOOD BACON

INGREDIENTS

- 1/2 of cup strawberry jam or preserves
- 1/4 of cup balsamic vinegar
- 1 teaspoon sriracha chili sauce
- 1 ball pizza dough your favorite
- 1 cup diced or shredded chicken breast from rotisserie chicken or left-over chicken of any kind
- 1/2 cup applewood smoked bacon cut in one-inch pieces, cooked and drained
- 1/2 cup thin sliced sweet onion
- 12 ounces shredded Italian blend cheese
- 1/4 cup fresh cilantro finely chopped
- 1/4 cup fresh strawberries diced small

INSTRUCTIONS

Place pizza stone or sheet pan on middle rack of oven. Preheat oven to 450 degrees F.

Place balsamic vinegar in a small saucepan. Bring to a boil, then reduce heat and simmer four to five minutes or until reduced to half of the original volume and mixture is thick and syrupy. Add strawberry preserves and Sriracha and mix well. Set aside to cool.

Pat or roll out pizza dough on a lightly floured surface to approximately a 14-inch circle. Shape does not have to be perfect; this is a rustic pizza. Place a piece of parchment paper, slightly larger than your dough on a pizza peel or an upside-down sheet pan. (The parchment paper will make your transfer of the pizza to the oven infinitely easier!) Sprinkle parchment paper lightly with cornmeal. Fold dough in quarters and place on parchment paper, then unfold.

Combine chicken with two tablespoons of the balsamic-strawberry mixture and mix to coat all chicken with sauce. Pour rest of sauce onto pizza dough and spread to cover. Leave a 1-inch border all around the edge. Scatter chicken evenly over the sauce.

Place about 3/4 of the cheese on top of dough and spread to cover sauce evenly. Scatter bacon and sweet onion over cheese to distribute evenly. Scatter remaining cheese over this layer.

Slide parchment paper with pizza on top onto stone or cookie sheet. Bake for approximately 8-10 minutes or until cheese is bubbly and crust is golden brown. Watch carefully, at this temperature it is easy to burn the pizza! Remove from oven and let cool slightly, 1-2 minutes. Sprinkle with chopped cilantro and fresh diced strawberries. Serve and enjoy!

4. RASPBERRY & MASCARPONE PIZZA

INGREDIENTS

- A pizza crust (homemade or store-bought)
- 1 tablespoon butter, melted
- Sugar for sprinkling
- 1/4 of cup lemon curd
- 1/2 of cup mascarpone cheese
- 2 tablespoons of powdered sugar, plus more for dusting
- 1/2 teaspoon of vanilla extract
- Fresh raspberries for sprinkling

INSTRUCTIONS

Preheat the oven to 450 degrees F. Roll out pizza dough and curl up edges to make a crust.

Brush middle of pizza dough with melted butter and sprinkle with sugar. Bake for about eight minutes or until golden brown.

Remove from oven and spread lemon curd on pizza crust. Bake 2 more minutes.

Allow crust to cool slightly. In the meantime, beat together mascarpone cheese, powdered sugar and vanilla extract. Once pizza has cooled, spread on top of lemon curd.

Spread as many raspberries as you want on top of the mascarpone cheese mixture. Sprinkle entire pizza with powdered sugar. Serve immediately.

5. GRILLED HONEY SRIRACHA CHICKEN PIZZA

INGREDIENTS

- 1 can (13.8 oz) Pillsbury™ Refrigerated Pizza Crust
- 2 tablespoons olive oil
- 1/4 cup honey
- 2 tablespoons orange marmalade
- 1 tablespoon soy sauce
- 2 teaspoons lime juice
- 4 tablespoons sriracha, divided
- 1 cup cooked chicken, shredded
- 1-2 cups Muir Glen™ organic tomato sauce
- 1 1/2 cups manchego cheese, shredded
- 1 cup mozzarella cheese, shredded
- 4 slices cooked bacon, crumbled
- 4 green onions, chopped
- Ranch dressing, for serving (optional)

INSTRUCTIONS

Preheat the grill to medium heat, and gather your ingredients.

Unroll the dough onto a heavily floured cookie sheet or pizza peel.

Spray the dough with cooking spray or rub olive oil over the dough.

Very carefully invert the dough from the pizza peel onto the grill. Grill 2-3 minutes; flip and grill another two minutes.

Remove crust from the grill and place back on the pizza peel or a baking sheet.

In a small saucepan combine the honey, soy sauce, orange marmalade, lime juice, and 2 tablespoons sriracha.

Bring to a boil and then reduce the heat. Simmer five minutes or until slightly thickened.

Once the sauce is thickened, remove from the heat and add the chicken. Toss well.

Cover the pizza in Muir Glen tomato sauce, then drizzle with sriracha to taste.

Add the manchego cheese. Then add the chicken mixture and all of the sauce that may be left in the pot. Add the crumbled bacon and mozzarella over the top.

Carefully slide the pizza back on the grill. Close grill cover and cook over low-medium heat for 5-8 minutes, or until the cheese is melted. Remove from the grill, slice and eat immediately.

6. CHIPOTLE CAJUN SHRIMP & GUACAMOLE PIZZA

INGREDIENTS

PIZZA DOUGH

- 1/2 cup warm water
- 1 1/2 teaspoons active dry yeast
- 1 tablespoon of honey
- 1 1/2 cups flour
- 1/4 teaspoon salt
- 1 tablespoon olive oil

GUACAMOLE

- 3 large hass avocados peeled, pitted and diced
- 1 jalapeno seeded and diced
- 1/4 cup fresh cilantro chopped
- 2 green onions, chopped
- 1 red pepper, chopped
- 2 whole sun-dried tomatoes, chopped
- 1 in canned chipotle chile adobo and 1 tablespoon adobo sauce
- 1/3 cup blue cheese or goat cheese, crumbled

CAJUN SHRIMP + PIZZA TOPPINGS

- 1 pound shrimp peeled and deveined
- 2 tablespoons olive oil
- 1 tablespoon cajun seasoning
- 1 tablespoon creole seasoning
- 1/2 tablespoon brown sugar
- 1 in canned chipotle chile adobo and 1 tablespoon adobo sauce
- 1/4 teaspoon salt and pepper plus more to taste
- 8 ounces sharp white cheddar cheese shredded
- 2 ounces blue cheese or goat cheese crumbled
- chopped green onions + cilantro for garnish

INSTRUCTIONS

For the Dough:

In a large bowl, combine water, yeast and honey. Mix with a spoon, then let sit until foamy, about ten minutes. Add in the one cup flour, the salt and olive oil stirring with a spoon until the dough comes together but is still sticky.

Using your hands, form the dough into a ball and work the additional 1/2 cup flour in to the dough if needed, kneading it on a floured surface for a few minutes.

You can also do all the mixing and kneading in your stand mixer with the dough hook attachment.

Rub the same bowl with olive oil then place the dough inside, turning to coat.

Cover with a towel and place in a warm place to rise for about 1 and a half hours.

When the dough is ready, start assembling the pizzas.

Preheat the oven to 375 degrees F.

To make the guacamole, add the avocado halves to a medium size mixing bowl.

Squeeze the lime juice over the avocados and toss well to coat.

Add in a pinch of cajun seasoning if desired.

Now grab a fork and lightly mash the avocados.

Next fold in the chopped jalapeno, cilantro, green onions, red pepper, sun-dried tomatoes, chipotle chile and adobo sauce and blue cheese (or goat cheese).

Add a pinch of salt and pepper.

Taste and season with more salt and pepper if desired.

Heat a medium skillet over medium heat.

In a bowl toss the shrimp with the olive oil, cajun seasoning, creole seasoning, brown sugar, chipotle chile and adobo sauce and a pinch of salt and pepper.

Add the shrimp to a skillet in a single layer and sear for three to four minutes, flip and sear another 3 minutes.

Try not to overcook the shrimp as it will continue to cook in the oven. Remove from the heat.

Grab the pizza dough and either leave the dough as one large (about 12-inch) pizza or divide it into three to four smaller pizzas.

Use your hands or a rolling pin to roll the dough out until you have a flattened disk.

Place the pizzas on a greased baking sheet and then use your hands to gently tug, pull and push the pizza dough into your desired shape.

Spread the pizzas with a layer of guacamole (do not use all the guacamole, save some for topping) and then spread the cheese over the guacamole add the shrimp and another sprinkle of cheese.

Bake the pizza for 25 to 30 minutes or until the cheese is all melty and gooey.

Remove and top with blue cheese (or goat cheese), dollops of the remaining guacamole, green onions and cilantro. Slice and eat!

7. CHEESY CRUNCHY NACHOS PIZZA

INGREDIENTS

- 1 Tablespoon of diced tomatoes (good drained)
- 1 cup of shredded cheese
- 1/4 cup of black beans
- 2 Tablespoons of pizza sauce
- 1 tube pizza crust
- 1 jalapeño
- 1/2 bag of tortilla chips

INSTRUCTIONS

Roll out dough on a nonstick cookie sheet.

Add a small amount of pizza sauce on the dough and lightly spread it around.

Place in the oven for seven minutes at 425 degrees F.

When the dough has cooked, take the pan out and turn on the broil to preheat.

Sprinkle the tortillas all over the pizza.

Add black beans, diced tomatoes, and cheese right on top.

Place in the broiler for a 1 or 2 minutes or until the cheese completely melts.

Take the pan out of the oven and sprinkle sliced jalapeños on top.

Serve immediately.

8. JALAPENO POPPER PIZZA

INGREDIENTS

- 4 slices bacon (diced)
- 2 tablespoons of olive oil
- 4 jalapeno chiles (sliced)
- 1 Thai red chili pepper (sliced)
- 1 shallot (sliced)
- 1/4 cup of yellow cornmeal
- 1 (13.8-ounce can) refrigerated classic pizza crust
- 1 (8-ounce) package cream cheese (at room temperature)
- 2 cups of shredded Monterey Jack cheese

INSTRUCTIONS

Preheat the oven to 450 degrees F.

Lightly coat a baking sheet or pizza pan with olive oil.

Heat a large skillet over medium high heat.

Add bacon and cook until brown and crispy, about six to eight minutes. Transfer to a paper towel-lined plate.

In a small bowl, combine olive oil, jalapeño, red chili pepper and shallot; set aside.

Working on a surface that has been sprinkled with cornmeal, roll out the pizza into a 12-inch-diameter round.

Transfer to prepared baking sheet or pizza pan.

Spread the cream cheese evenly over the top, leaving a 1-inch border.

Top with bacon, jalapeño mixture and cheese.

Place into the oven and bake for 15-20 minutes, or until the crust is golden brown and the cheese has melted.

Serve immediately.

9. TACO PIZZA

INGREDIENTS

- 1/3 pizza dough from this recipe
- 1 cup refried beans
- 1 lb ground beef extra lean
- 1 tbsp olive oil
- 2 cups cheddar cheese shredded
- 1 small onion chopped
- 2 cloves garlic minced
- 2 tbsp taco seasoning

Optional Toppings

- 1/2 cup iceberg lettuce
- 1/2 cup tomatoes
- 1/4 cup black olives
- 1/4 cup green onions
- 1/2 cup salsa
- sour cream

INSTRUCTIONS

Preheat oven to 500 F.

Roll out the pizza dough and place it on a baking dish or pizza stone.

Bake the pizza dough for about 5 to 7 minutes, just until it starts to get lightly golden.

In the meantime, add the olive oil to a skillet; when oil is hot, add onion and garlic and sauté until onion is translucent.

Add ground beef to skillet and taco seasoning. Cook until beef is cooked through.

Spread the refried beans over the pizza dough, next top with the ground beef mixture; add shredded cheese.

Put pizza back in the oven and bake for an additional five to ten minutes or until cheese has melted and crust is golden.

Finish the pizza off with the rest of the toppings, lettuce, tomatoes, green onions and olives.

Serve with salsa and sour cream if preferred.

10. BLACKBERRY RICOTTA PIZZA + BASIL

INGREDIENTS

- 1 tablespoon of olive oil
- 1/2 cup of fresh blackberries (smashed)
- 1 cup of Parmesan (shredded)
- 1 cup of swiss cheese or mozzarella (shredded)
- 3/4 cup ricotta
- 1/2 cup blackberries, whole
- 1/4 cup green onions, chopped
- 1/2 teaspoon salt, more to taste
- ground pepper to taste (I like lots)
- 2-3 tablespoons fresh basil, chopped

INSTRUCTIONS

Preheat your oven to 450 F. Put your pizza stone in the oven if you have one.

Roll out your pizza dough on a floured sheet of parchment paper to about 12 inches. (If you don't have a pizza stone, you should probably transfer the dough to a baking sheet now.)

Drizzle one tablespoon of olive oil over the top of the dough and use your fingers or a pastry brush to coat well, especially the edges.

Use a fork to mash a half cup of blackberries in a bowl. It doesn't have to be perfect. Use the fork or a slotted spoon to ladle the pulp onto the pizza. Spread it around like you would pizza sauce. (You don't need the remaining juice, but don't throw it out. Drink that sweet nectar if you know what's good for you.)

Top the smashed berries with one cup of Parmesan and one cup swiss or mozzarella, making sure to get the crust.

Use a spoon to dollop the ricotta over the pizza. It doesn't have to be perfect.

Top with whole fresh blackberries and chopped green onions.

Sprinkle with salt, and add pepper to taste.

When the oven is hot, transfer the pizza to the oven. I transfer it using a a flat baking sheet, still on the parchment paper.

Bake for about eight to ten minutes, or until the top has started to brown. You can broil it for a minute if you want it crispier on top.

Remove from the oven and immediately sprinkle some chopped basil on top.

Slice and enjoy!

11. MARINATED KALE & WHIPPED RICOTTA PIZZA

INGREDIENTS

PIZZA DOUGH

- 1 1/8 cups of warm water
- 3 teaspoons active dry yeast
- 1 tablespoon honey
- 1 tablespoon olive oil
- 3 cups all-purpose flour
- 1 teaspoon salt

PIZZA

- 1 head of kale, stems removed
- 2 tablespoons chili garlic paste
- 1 tablespoon olive oil
- 1 tablespoon honey
- 1 1/2 cups ricotta cheese
- 1/3 cup finely grated parmigiano-regianno cheese, plus more for sprinkling
- 1/4 teaspoon salt
- 1/4 teaspoon pepper
- 6 ounces fontina cheese, freshly grated
- crushed red pepper flakes for topping

INSTRUCTIONS

FOR THE DOUGH

In a large bowl, combine water, yeast, honey and olive oil. Mix with a spoon, then let sit until foamy, about ten minutes.

Add in 2 and 1/2 cups flour and salt, stirring with a spoon until the dough comes together but is still sticky. Using your hands, form the dough into a ball and work in the additional 1/2 cup flour, kneading it on a floured surface for a few minutes.

Rub the same bowl with olive oil then place the dough inside, turning to coat. Cover with a towel and place in a warm place to rise for about 1-1 1/2 hours.

After the dough has risen, punch it down and place it back on the floured surface. Using a rolling pin or your hands, form it into your desired and place on a baking sheet or pizza peel.

Place the towel back over the dough and let sit in the warm place for ten minutes.

Preheat oven to 425 degrees F.

NOTE: If you use my pizza stone, heat the oven to 475 degrees F and bake for 15 minutes. If you're just using a baking sheet, follow the directions below for baking and set to 425 degrees.

FOR THE PIZZA

Chop the kale into slices and shreds with your knife, then place it in a bowl.

Add the olive oil, honey and chili garlic paste then toss well to coat. Massage with your hands for two to three minutes, then let it sit until ready to use.

Add the ricotta to a food processor and blend until it's smooth and creamy.

Add in the cheese, salt and pepper, pureeing again until combined.

Brush the pizza dough with the olive oil. Spread 1/2 of the whipped ricotta on the dough, leaving a 1/2-inch at the edge of the crust.

Cover the ricotta with the shredded kale, then add scoops of the leftover ricotta on top of the kale randomly.

Sprinkle the fontina on top.

Bake for 25-30 minutes (or a little less if using the stone) or until the cheese is golden and bubbly.

Remove and let cool slightly before serving.

Top with the extra Parmigiano-Reggiano and crushed red pepper flakes.

12. SAUSAGE, APPLE & THYME BREAKFAST PIZZA

INGREDIENTS

- 1 pound of pizza dough
- 1 cup of shredded part skim mozzarella cheese
- 1/2 cup of shredded smoked gouda cheese
- 1 link cooked chicken apple sausage (sliced thin)

APPLE AND ONION SAUTÉ

- 1 gala or similar apple (sliced thin)
- 1 small yellow onion (sliced thin)
- Kosher salt & fresh ground black pepper to taste

SCRAMBLED EGGS

- 3 eggs
- 4 egg whites
- Kosher salt & fresh ground black pepper to taste
- 1 teaspoon of chopped fresh thyme leaves

DIJON MUSTARD SAUCE

- 2 teaspoons of low-fat mayonnaise
- 2 teaspoon of dijon mustard
- Kosher salt & fresh ground black pepper to taste

INSTRUCTIONS

Preheat oven to 400-degree F.

Roll or stretch the pizza dough onto a pizza stone of baking sheet sprayed with cooking spray.

Bake the pizza dough for 10 minutes then remove it from the oven.

In a small bowl whisk together the Dijon mustard sauce, set aside.

Heat a medium sized skillet over medium high heat and spray it generously with cooking spray.

Add in the thinly sliced onion along with a pinch of salt and sauté for about four minutes stirring the onions a couple times.

After four minutes add in the thinly sliced apple and sauté another three minutes until the apple has softened slightly and the onions are soft and golden.

Remove the cooked onion and apple from the pan onto a plate, set aside.

In a large bowl whisk together the eggs, egg whites, salt, pepper, and thyme.

In the same skillet over medium heat spray again with more cooking spray.

Pour the egg mixture into the prepared skillet and scramble the eggs just until they are set, about three minutes.

ASSEMBLING THE PIZZA

Once the pizza dough has baked for ten minutes remove it from the oven and spread the Dijon mustard sauce all over the top.

Take half of the shredded cheese and sprinkle it over the baked pizza dough.

Spread the scrambled eggs, apple and onion mixture, sliced sausage, and remaining cheese all over the top of the pizza.

Place the pizza back in the oven and bake for an additional six to ten minutes or until the cheese is melted and bubbly.

Remove the pizza from the oven and sprinkle with chopped fresh thyme.

13. FAMOUS SHRIMP FRA DIAVOLO PIZZA

INGREDIENTS

- 1 medium pizza dough, homemade or store-bought
- 1/4 cup or 4 Tbsp. olive oil, divided
- 1 lb. of large uncooked shrimp, peeled and deveined
- pinch of salt and black pepper
- 5 cloves garlic (minced)
- 1 medium onion (thinly sliced)
- 1 cup of dry white or red wine
- 2 cups of grape tomatoes (halved)
- 1 tsp. of crushed red pepper flakes
- 1/4 tsp. of dried oregano
- 2 cups of shredded mozzarella cheese
- 1/2 cup of fresh basil (chopped)
- Grated Parmesan cheese

INSTRUCTIONS

Preheat oven (and baking stone if using) to 425 F.

Heat one Tbsp. oil in a large skillet over medium-high heat. Season shrimp with salt and pepper, then add to the skillet.

Sauté for one minute, then flip shrimp and sauté until the shrimp is just seared on both sides. Remove and transfer shrimp to a separate plate.

Add an additional two Tbsp. oil to the skillet. Add onions & sauté for another five minutes, or until translucent.

Add garlic and sauté for one minute. Add wine, and deglaze pan for one minute. Then add tomatoes, crushed red pepper, and oregano.

Reduce heat to medium-low, and let simmer and reduce for 10-15 minutes, stirring occasionally. Remove from heat and set aside.

Meanwhile, brush or mist the top of the pizza crust with the remaining one Tbsp. oil.

Sprinkle about half of the mozzarella cheese evenly over the top of the pizza, leaving a 1-inch border.

Then evenly spread the tomato mixture on top of the cheese. Add the shrimp in an even layer, and then cover with the remaining mozzarella.

Bake for about ten to twelve minutes, or until dough has risen and cheese is melted. Remove and garnish with chopped fresh basil and Parmesan cheese. Serve immediately.

14. RHUBARB BASIL PIZZA + APPLE HONEY BBQ SAUCE

INGREDIENTS

- prepared pizza dough for 1 13-14" pizza pan
- 1 tsp cornmeal
- 1/4 cup sweet BBQ sauce (I used the Apple Honey BBQ sauce in recipe below)
- 1 Tbsp Olive Oil
- 3 green onions chopped *or* 1/2 med onion minced
- 3 decent sized stalks of rhubarb
- 1/4 cup basil, chopped, plus a small handful more (not chopped) for garnish
- 125g Goat Cheese (1/2 regular sized package)
- 1/2 cup shredded Mozzarella cheese

INSTRUCTIONS

Preheat the oven to 425 F.

Heat olive oil in a skillet on med-low heat. When the oil starts to shimmer, add onions, saute for two minutes.

Chop rhubarb into 1/4" pieces and add to onions. Saute for two more minutes.

Remove from heat, set aside.

Grease your pizza pan with olive oil, and sprinkle the cornmeal evenly over the pan (this prevents the crust from sticking to the pan).

Stretch the dough out in the pan and spread evenly with BBQ sauce.

Apply your toppings evenly over the sauce: first the onion/rhubarb mix, then the basil, then the goat cheese, and finally the mozzarella.

Bake in preheated oven for 10 minutes, or until crust is starting to become golden.

Add a minute or two at a time so you don't over-do it.

Top with basil leaf garnish, serve hot.

NOTES: While other sweet BBQ sauces would work well, I think you'll have the best taste results if you use the Apple Honey BBQ sauce.

15. DEEP DISH APPLE PIZZA

INGREDIENTS

- 13.5 oz. Can of Pizza Dough
- 4 tbsp. of unsalted butter, divided
- 2 tbsp. sugar
- 1/2 tsp. of cinnamon
- 3 Granny Smith Apples, peeled and sliced
- 1/4 c. of brown sugar
- 1/2 tsp. cinnamon
- Crumble topping
- 1/3 c. of sugar
- 1/3 c. of brown sugar
- 1 tsp. of cinnamon
- 1/4 tsp. of salt
- 1 stick unsalted butter, melted
- 1 1/2 c. of flour
- Glaze
- 1 1/2 c. powdered sugar
- 2 tbsp. Milk

INSTRUCTIONS

Melt 2 tbsp. butter in a medium sized skillet. Add the apples to the pan and allow them to cook for 5 minutes.

Add the brown sugar and cinnamon and stir and cook for another ten minutes so the apples can cook and slightly thicken. Remove from heat and allow to cool completely.

Preheat oven to 425: Meanwhile, spray a 9 inch round pan or cast iron skillet in equal size with baking spray.

Open the pizza dough and place the dough inside of the pan working the dough along the sides of the pan and cutting off any excess dough that may be hanging from the pan.

Melt the last 2 tbsp of butter and brush the entire dough.

Combine the 2 tbsp sugar and 1/2 tsp of cinnamon and sprinkle evenly across the dough and on the sides.

Combine the sugar, brown sugar, cinnamon, salt, and melted butter in a bowl. Add the flour an stir until well mixed and crumbly.

Spread the crumble mixture on parchment or wax paper an allow to sit for 10 minutes.

Now, add the apples to spread on top of the dough. Use a serrated spoon so you are not adding excess liquid from the apples.

Spread the crumble mixture on top of the apples evenly (we didn't use all of the crumble mixture but that is up to you).

Bake for 8-10 minutes until the crust or until the crust is golden brown.

Mix the powdered sugar and milk in a small bowl and grizzle on top of the pizza.

Allow to cool slightly and serve.

16. CHICKEN ENCHILADA PIZZA

INGREDIENTS

DOUGH

- 1 1/8 cups of warm water
- 3 teaspoons of active dry yeast
- 1 tablespoon of honey
- 1 tablespoon of olive oil
- 3 cups of all-purpose flour
- 1 teaspoon of salt

PIZZA

- 2 boneless, skinless chicken breasts, cooked and shredded
- 1 tablespoon of olive oil
- 1/2 of red onion, diced
- 1/2 of red pepper, diced
- 1/2 of green pepper, diced
- 1/2 of jalapeño, seeded and diced
- 2 of garlic cloves, minced
- 1 (or 4 ounce) can of diced green chiles
- 1 of teaspoon ground cumin
- 1 of teaspoon smoked paprika
- 1 teaspoon chili powder
- 1 cup of enchilada sauce
- 6 ounces sharp cheddar cheese (freshly grated)
- 6 ounces monterey jack cheese (freshly grated)
- 1 cup of grape tomatoes, quarted
- 1 cup of shredded lettuce
- 1 avocado, thinly sliced
- Sour cream or greek yogurt for topping

INSTRUCTIONS

DOUGH

In a large bowl, combine water, yeast, honey and olive oil.

Mix with a spoon, then let sit until foamy, about ten minutes.

Add in 2 1/2 cups flour and salt, stirring with a spoon until the dough comes together but it still sticky.

Using your hands, form the dough into a ball and work in the additional 1/2 cup flour, kneading it on a floured surface for a few minutes.

Rub the same bowl with olive oil then place the dough inside, turning to coat. Cover with a towel and place in a warm place to rise for about 1-1 1/2 hours.

After the dough has risen, punch it down and place it back on the floured surface. Using a rolling pin or your hands, form it into your desired and place on a baking sheet or pizza peel.

Place the towel back over the dough and let sit in the warm place for 10 minutes.

PIZZA

Preheat oven to 375 degrees F. (We actually used a pizza stone and heated my oven to 450 degrees F, and baked for 15 minutes).

If you're just using a baking sheet, follow the directions below for baking and set to 375 degrees F.)

Heat a large skillet over medium-low heat and add olive oil.

Add in onions, garlic and peppers with a pinch of salt and stir well.

Cook until soft, about five minutes.

Toss in shredded chicken with green chiles, cumin, paprika and chili powder.

Stir to coat well and cook for another 5 minutes. Turn off heat.

Spread a a thin layer – about 1/2 cup – of enchilada sauce all over the pizza dough.

Cover in a small sprinkle of cheese, then top with the chicken and pepper mixture. Add remaining cheese on top evenly.

Place in the oven and bake for 25-30 minutes, until cheese and crust is golden and bubbly. Remove and let cool for fine to ten minutes, then top with lettuce, tomatoes and avocado.

Serve with an extra drizzle of enchilada sauce and sour cream or greek yogurt.

17. BEER-BATTERED FRIED CALAMARI PIZZA

INGREDIENTS (for two pizzas)

For the dough:

- 1 (1/4th oz) packet dry active yeast
- 3/4 cup of warm water
- 1 Tbs. sugar
- 1 tsp of salt
- 1/8 cup of olive oil
- 2 cups of all-purpose flour, plus more for the work surface

For the calamari:

- 1 pound of calamari rings
- 3 cups favorite seafood batter mix, divided. You can also use a mix of flour, cayenne, salt and pepper.
- 1 cup of beer
- 4 cups of canola oil

For the rest:

- 1 cup of favorite pizza sauce
- A good handful sliced pepperoncini (banana peppers)
- 3 cups shredded of fresh mozzarella (or a block is fine)
- minced parsley
- 1 lemon, zested
- 1/2 cup Greek yogurt
- 2 tsp hot sauce (like Tabasco)
- 2 tsp juice from the pepperoncini jar

INSTRUCTIONS

Start your dough. Pour the warm water into a large bowl and add the yeast. Let sit for five minutes until it gets bubbly.

Whisk in the sugar, salt and oil. Then add the two cups of flour. Mix until you get a soft gooey ball of dough.

Remove the ball of dough from the bowl, wipe it out, place it back and brush with a little bit of olive oil.

Cover with a clean kitchen towel and let rest for an hour, until doubled in size.

While the dough rests, start on your calamari. Bring the oil to a pipin' 350 degrees F in a straight-sided pan.

In a small bowl, combine one cup of the batter mix with the one cup of beer.

Place the rest of the batter mix in another shallow dish.

In a few small batches dredge the calamari rings through the beer batter, shake off any excess goo, then toss them around in the remaining dry mix.

Fry in batches until golden brown, draining on a plate with paper towels.

Preheat your oven to 400 F. Stick a pizza stone in there if you have one!

Divide the pizza dough into two balls and roll them out until you get a good 9-inch or 10-inch pizza.

Spoon as much sauce as you like over each crust. Follow with a scattering of banana peppers and mozzarella cheese.

Slide into the oven and bake for about 15 minutes, allowing the crust to brown and the cheese to bubble up with glory.

While the pizza is baking, mix together the yogurt, hot sauce and pepperoncini juice.

Remove from the oven and top with fried calamari, a healthy drizzle of the cream sauce, minced parsley and lemon zest.

Serve with lemon wedges

18. GRILLED PEACH PIZZA + PROSCIUTTO

INGREDIENTS

- 2 peaches (cut into 1/2-inch wedges)
- 1-pound fresh mozzarella cheese (thinly sliced)
- 3 Grilled Pizza Dough crusts
- 12 thin slices of prosciutto (cut in half)
- 1/3 cup of fresh basil
- Extra-virgin olive oil (for drizzling)

INSTRUCTIONS

Heat grill to high.

Grill peach wedges, flipping, until caramelized, about two minutes per side.

Preheat oven to 400 degrees F (or heat grill to medium).

Sprinkle cheese on grilled pizza crusts.

Bake or grill, covered with lid, directly on grates, until cheese melts and is bubbling, about eight minutes (time may vary slightly if grilling).

Remove from oven or grill.

Top with peaches, prosciutto, and basil.

Drizzle with oil.

19. CHOCOLATE RASPBERRY PIZZA

INGREDIENTS

FOR THE CHOCOLATE COOKIE DOUGH:

- 2 tablespoons of butter, softened
- 2 tablespoons of white sugar
- 1 large of egg yolk
- 1/4 teaspoon of vanilla extract
- 1/4 cup of flour
- 3 tablespoons of cocoa powder
- 1/8 teaspoon of baking powder

FOR THE REST:

- 1/4 cup of chocolate chips
- 2 tablespoons of shredded coconut, toasted
- 2 tablespoons of slivered almonds, toasted
- handful fresh raspberries (washed & dried)
- 1 oz. Of real white chocolate, melted

INSTRUCTIONS

Preheat the oven to 350-degree F.

First, make the crust: In a small bowl, stir together the butter, sugar, egg yolk and vanilla. Stir the mixture very well, smearing the sugar into the butter until it's well-blended.

Sprinkle the flour, cocoa powder and baking powder on top. Stir until just combined, but don't over-mix.

Scoop the mixture out onto a cookie sheet lined with parchment or a silicone liner.

Shape the mixture into a 6" round disc, and then use your fingers to gently make a slight lip on the edge.

Bake for nine minutes. Remove the cookie from the oven, sprinkle the chocolate chips on top, and immediately return it to the oven.

Let it bake one minute more to melt the chocolate chips.

When you remove the cookie from the oven, the chips won't look melted: use a knife to spread them and they will melt easily.

Top the pizza with the coconut, almonds and raspberries. Drizzle the white chocolate on top. Serve in slices.

20. BACON & EGGS BREAKFAST PIZZA WITH HASHBROWN CRUST

INGREDIENTS

HASHBROWN CRUST:

- 4 cups of frozen seasoned hashbrowns, thawed
- 1/2 Teaspoon of smoked paprika
- 1/4 Teaspoon of black pepper
- 2 eggs
- 1 1/2 cups grated cheese (4 ounces)

TOPPINGS:

- 6 strips of bacon, cut into bite sized pieces (6 ounces)
- 6 eggs
- 1 cup of grated cheese (2 1/2 ounces)

FRESH TOPPINGS:

- 1 cup of thinly sliced green onions (about 1/2 a bunch)
- 1 cup of diced tomatoes, or halved cherry tomatoes
- 1/2 of ripe avocado, thinly sliced or cubed
- Sriracha to taste

INSTRUCTIONS

Preheat the oven to 400 F and line a baking sheet with parchment paper.

Mix together all the ingredients for the hash brown crust in a bowl until combined.

Pat the mixture into a crust shape about 1/2" thick and 10-12" in diameter, making small ridges around the edge as you go.

Bake the crust for 20-25 minutes, or until golden brown.

While the crust bakes, fry the bacon pieces until they're crispy, drain and set aside.

Prepare your choice of the fresh toppings, and set them aside.

When the crust is done, take it out of the oven and sprinkle the bacon bits over the top.

Crack the eggs one at a time into a small dish, and then carefully place the eggs as evenly as you can around the pizza.

Top with the grated cheese, and bake again until the eggs are your desired doneness, about 6-8 minutes for over easy eggs.

Remove the pizza from the oven and top with the fresh toppings.

Serve immediately. If you do have any leftovers, remove any avocado before refrigerating them (the avocado turns brown).

Then reheat the leftovers gently at 300 F until warm.

The eggs get a little firmer but otherwise it's still delicious.

21. GREEK PIZZA

INGREDIENTS

- 16 oz pizza dough, homemade or store-bought
- 2 1/2 Tbsp of extra virgin olive oil, divided
- 3 of garlic cloves, minced
- 1/2 tsp of dried oregano
- 1/4 tsp of dried basil
- 1/8 tsp of dried thyme
- Salt and freshly ground black pepper
- 6 oz of fresh mozzarella, chopped into pieces (regular low moisture mozzarella would be fine too)
- 4 oz of Greek feta cheese, crumbled
- 1/2 cup of chopped bell pepper (any variety)
- 1 cup of diced grape tomatoes, halved
- 1/3 cup of chopped Greek Kalamata olives or black olives
- 1/4 cup of chopped red onion
- 1 tbsp of chopped fresh parsley

INSTRUCTIONS

Preheat your oven to 450 degrees F.

Place pizza stone in oven and rest 30 minutes. Meanwhile combine 1 1/2 tbsp olive oil and garlic in a small bowl.

Spread and shape pizza crust into a 12 to 13-inch round over a sheet of lightly floured parchment paper, while creating a rim along edge of dough.

Brush pizza dough evenly with olive oil mixture.

Sprinkle evenly with oregano, basil, thyme (leaving rim uncovered with herbs) and season lightly with salt and pepper.

Top evenly with mozzarella and Greek feta cheese.

Bake in preheated oven 12 - 15 minutes until crust is golden.

Meanwhile, sauté peppers in a skillet in one tbsp olive oil over medium high heat until tender (*you could also just add them on without sauteing*).

Remove pizza from oven and immediately top with peppers, tomatoes, olives, onion and parsley.

Cut into slices and serve.

22. MEATBALL CARAMELIZED ONION PIZZA

INGREDIENTS

- 2 tablespoons of unsalted butter
- 1 bunch of asparagus (sliced)
- 1 teaspoon of salt
- teaspoons freshly ground black pepper (for taste)
- 1 pre-cooked pizza shell (large)
- 1 package Chicken Meatballs, Caramelized Onion
- 1/2 cup of crumbled goat cheese
- 1/2 cup of sliced figs
- 2 tablespoons of olive oil
- 1 bunch of arugula (washed and dried)

INSTRUCTIONS

Preheat oven to 450 F.

Melt the butter in a large, heavy-bottomed skillet.

Add the sliced figs and cook slowly over low heat, turn occasionally until lightly caramelized, about ten minutes.

Set aside.

Brush the pizza shell with olive oil and arrange the meatball slices and asparagus on the pizza shell.

Finish with cheese, figs and arugula.

Bake for ten to fifteen minutes.

23. MONKEY PIZZA BREAD PLUS ROSEMARY

INGREDIENTS

- 20 gr of baker's yeast
- 1 salt (level tablespoon)
- 1 tablespoon sugar
- 300 milliliters water (tepid)
- 500 gr of flour
- 70 gr of ham (diced white, or bacon, blanched before)
- 150 grams of grated cheese
- olive oil
- rosemary
- salt (Espelette pepper)
- 450 gr of pizza sauce (tomato, for dipping)

INSTRUCTIONS

In the mixer bowl, put the yeast, salt, sugar, and half water. Mix with a fork.

Add the flour and knead for sever to nine minutes to get a very soft dough.

Cover with plastic film and let rise for 30 minutes until it doubles its size.

On a floured work surface drop your dough and cut it into small balls of about 25-grams each.

Flatten each ball, drop cubes of ham and a little bit of grated cheese in the center.

Close these balls by forming amonieres.

Grease a kouglof pan and drop a first row of balls. Brush them with olive oil, and sprinkle them with some rosemary.

Sprinkle a little salt or spices or herbs between each row.

Continue to fill the mold with the remaining dough balls.

Let stand for 25 minutes while you preheat oven to 180 degrees Celsius.

Bake 25 to 30 minutes.

Wait five minutes before turning out onto a rack. Serve warm with a sauce tomato pizza.

24. THAI PORK PIZZA

INGREDIENTS

- 2 boneless pork chops (3/4-inch thick)
- 2 teaspoons of vegetable oil
- 15 ounces of pizza crust (Boboli)
- 1/2 cup of peanut sauce (Thai)
- 1 cup of mozzarella cheese (shredded)
- 1/2 cup of pea pods (thinly sliced)
- 1/4 cup of carrots (shredded)
- cilantro leaves (chopped, if desired)

INSTRUCTIONS

Heat the oven to 425 degrees F.

Place the pizza crust on a baking sheet.

Spread the peanut sauce onto the crust. Sprinkle with pea pods and carrots.

Heat the oil in a nonstick skillet and heat over medium-high heat. Sprinkle the pork chops with salt and pepper.

Add the pork chops to the skillet and cook 4 minutes until browned and internal temperature reaches 145 degrees F, followed by a three-minute rest time.

Cut into thin slices. Arrange on the pizza crust. Cover with cheese.

Bake 12 to 14 minutes or until the cheese is melted and bubbly.

Let stand five minutes before slicing. Sprinkle with chopped cilantro if desired.

25. SWEET PIZZA WITH NECTARINES & BLUEBERRIES

INGREDIENTS

- 10 strawberries
- 110 grams of granulated sugar
- 1 tablespoon of rose water
- 150 grams of mascarpone
- 1 pizza dough
- 4 nectarines
- 125 grams of blueberries
- mint leaves

INSTRUCTIONS

Preheat oven to 410 degrees F.

Rinse and hull the strawberries. Place them in the bowl of a food processor.

Mix them with 100 gr of sugar, rose water, and mascarpone.

Unroll the pizza dough on a baking sheet lined with parchment paper. Prick it with a fork.

Spread the strawberry cream over the dough, leaving a border of 1 centimeter.

Rinse the nectarines and dry them with paper towel.

Cut them in half, remove the pit, and cut into slices. Place the slices over the dough.

Add the blueberries.

Sprinkle with the remaining sugar.

Cook for about twenty minutes.

Before serving, add small mint leaves.

26. MAN'OUCHE LEBANESE PIZZA

INGREDIENTS

- 50 milliliters of warm water
- 3 tablespoons of virgin olive oil
- 1/2 teaspoon salt
- 240 grams of Greek yogurt
- 310 grams of wheat flour
- 1 teaspoon of yeast (dehydrated)
- 1 teaspoon of granulated sugar
- 3 tablespoons za'atar
- 1 tablespoon spice (ground sumac)
- 80 milliliters of olive oil

INSTRUCTIONS

If you have a bread machine, first put water, oil, salt and yogurt, then the remaining ingredients and run the "dough cycle" program.

If you do not have a bread machine, mix the flour and salt in a large bowl.

In a medium-sized bowl, mix the yogurt and the oil and in another bowl, the water, the yeast and the sugar.

Make a well in the center of the flour pour the water-based mixture and then the yogurt mixture.

Mix all the ingredients with your fingertips, then knead for ten minutes. The dough should be soft and smooth.

Cover the dough and let it rise for at least 2 hours.

Preheat oven to 425 degrees F.

Mix together all the ingredients of the filling.

Line a baking sheet with parchment paper.

Divide the dough into several small balls, the size of an apricot.

Flatten each ball by hand, giving it a shape of a small pizza.

Arrange them on the baking sheet.

With a spoon, spread a little of the mixture for topping on each pizza. Put them in the oven for five to ten minutes.

The dough should not be too brown and must remain moist.

27. ANCIENT ROMAN PIZZA

INGREDIENTS

- 1/2 kilo spelt flour
- 300 milliliters of water
- 15 gr dry active yeast (instant)
- 1 teaspoon of sea salt
- 1 handful Greek feta cheese (crumbled)
- 1 tablespoon of sesame seeds
- 1 tablespoon of honey

INSTRUCTIONS

Mix together the flour, water, yeast, and salt. Knead about ten minutes until the glutens form.

You should be able to pinch off a section of dough and stretch it between your two hands without it breaking.

Make a ball with the dough and transfer it to a greased bowl. Turn the dough in the bowl until all sides are oiled. Cover with plastic wrap and let double in volume.

Once doubled, turn out onto a lightly floured work surface and form a roll or tube with the dough. Cut into 5 equal parts.

This will produce five pizzas 20 centimeters in diameter. *If you like bigger pizzas, cut accordingly but remember, they should be able to fit in your skillet.*

Any sections you do not plan to use immediately, wrap in plastic wrap and freeze for later.

Preheat the broiler of your oven.

Roll out the dough section to about twenty centimeters.

Place a large skillet on low heat and drizzle on olive oil. Once hot, add the rolled-out dough. It will start to inflate.

Once the bottom is golden, drizzle olive oil over the top and flip it. Remove from heat once both sides are golden.

Top the pizza with feta and sesame seeds and transfer to the oven.

When the feta cheese has softened (it will not melt), remove the pizza from the oven and drizzle on the honey.

28. ARUGULA & MUSHROOM BREAKFAST PIZZA

INGREDIENTS

- A prebaked 12-inch thin whole wheat pizza crust
- 3/4 cup of reduced-fat ricotta cheese
- 1 teaspoon of garlic powder
- 1 teaspoon of paprika, divided
- 1 cup of sliced baby portobello mushrooms
- 1/2 cup of julienned soft sun-dried tomatoes (*not packed in oil*)
- 3 cups of fresh arugula or baby spinach
- 2 tablespoons of balsamic vinegar
- 2 tablespoons of olive oil
- 1/4 teaspoon of salt, divided
- 1/4 teaspoon of pepper, divided
- 6 eggs (large)

INSTRUCTIONS

Preheat oven to 450 F.

Place crust on a pizza pan. Spread with ricotta cheese; sprinkle with garlic powder and a half teaspoon of paprika.

Top with mushrooms and tomatoes.

With clean hands, massage arugula with vinegar, oil and 1/8 teaspoon each salt and pepper until softened; arrange over pizza.

Using a spoon, make six indentations in arugula; carefully break an egg into each.

Sprinkle with the remaining paprika, salt and pepper.

Bake until egg whites are completely set and yolks begin to thicken but are not hard, 12 to 15 minutes.

29. DILL PICKLE HAMBURGER PIZZA

INGREDIENTS

- 1/2-pound ground beef
- A prebaked 12-inch pizza crust
- 1/2 cup of ketchup
- 1/4 cup of prepared mustard
- 1 & 1/2 cups of shredded cheddar cheese
- 2 cups of shredded lettuce
- 1/2 cup of chopped dill pickle
- 1/4 cup of chopped onion
- 1/2 cup of mayonnaise
- 2-3 tablespoons of dill pickle juice

INSTRUCTIONS

Preheat oven to 425-degree F.

In a large skillet, cook and crumble beef over medium heat until no longer pink, three to four minutes; drain.

Meanwhile, place crust on an ungreased baking sheet or pizza pan.

Mix ketchup and mustard; spread over crust.

Add ground beef; bake five minutes.

Sprinkle with cheese; bake until cheese is bubbly and crust is lightly browned, eight to ten minutes longer.

Top with lettuce, pickle and onion.

Whisk mayonnaise and enough pickle juice to reach desired consistency; pour over pizza.

30. BAKED POTATO PIZZA

INGREDIENTS

- 1 package (6 ounces) of pizza crust mix
- 3 medium unpeeled potatoes (baked and cooled)
- 1 tablespoon of butter (melted)
- 1/4 teaspoon of garlic powder
- 1/4 teaspoon of Italian seasoning or dried oregano
- One cup sour cream
- Six bacon strips (cooked and crumbled)
- 3 to 5 green onions (chopped)
- 1 & 1/2 cups of shredded mozzarella cheese
- 1/2 cup of shredded cheddar cheese

INSTRUCTIONS

Prepare crust according to package directions.

Press dough into a lightly greased 14-in. pizza pan; build up edges slightly.

Bake at 400 F for five to six minutes or until crust is firm and begins to brown.

Cut potatoes into 1/2-in. cubes.

In a bowl, combine butter, garlic powder and Italian seasoning.

Add potatoes and toss.

Spread sour cream over crust; top with potato mixture, bacon, onions and cheeses.

Bake at 400 F for 15-20 minutes or until cheese is lightly browned.

Let stand for five minutes before cutting.

31. CALIFORNIA CLUB PIZZA

INGREDIENTS

- 1 tablespoon of cornmeal
- A portion (1 lb.) of Whole Wheat Pizza Dough
- 1/2 cup of shredded reduced-fat Mexican cheese blend
- 3 bacon of strips, cooked and crumbled
- 3 cups of shredded romaine
- 1/4 cup of fat-free mayonnaise
- 1 tablespoon lime juice
- 3 teaspoons of minced fresh cilantro, divided
- 1 cup of alfalfa sprouts
- 1 medium tomato, thinly sliced
- 1/2 medium of ripe avocado, peeled and cut into eight slices

INSTRUCTIONS

Coat a 12-in. pizza pan with cooking spray; sprinkle with cornmeal.

On a floured surface, roll dough into a 13-in. circle.

Transfer to prepared pan; build up edges slightly.

Sprinkle with cheese and bacon.

Bake at 450-degree F for ten to twelve minutes or until crust is lightly browned.

Meanwhile, place romaine in a large bowl.

In a small bowl, combine the mayonnaise, lime juice and 2 teaspoons cilantro.

Pour over romaine; toss to coat.

Arrange over warm pizza. Top with sprouts, tomato, avocado and remaining cilantro.

Serve immediately.

32. CHICKEN CAESAR PIZZA

INGREDIENTS

- 1 tube (13.8 ounces) of refrigerated pizza crust
- 1 tablespoon of olive oil
- 1-pound of boneless skinless chicken breasts, cut into half-inch cubes
- 1-1/2 teaspoons minced garlic, divided
- 6 tablespoons of creamy Caesar salad dressing, divided
- 2 cups of shredded Monterey Jack cheese
- 1/2 cup of grated Parmesan cheese
- 2 cups of hearts of romaine salad mix
- 2 green onions, thinly sliced
- 2 plum tomatoes, chopped

INSTRUCTIONS

Preheat oven to 400-degree F.

Unroll pizza crust and press to fit into a greased 15x10x1-in. baking pan, pinching edges to form a rim.

Bake ten minutes or until edges are lightly browned.

Meanwhile, in a large skillet, heat oil over medium-high heat.

Add chicken & 1/2 teaspoon garlic; cook and stir until chicken is no longer pink.

Remove from heat; stir in two tablespoons salad dressing.

Spread crust with 3 tablespoons salad dressing; sprinkle with remaining garlic.

Top with half of the cheeses and all of the chicken. Sprinkle with remaining cheeses.

Bake for 10-15 minutes or until crust is golden brown and cheese is melted.

In a small bowl, toss salad mix and green onions with remaining dressing.

Just before serving, top pizza with salad and tomatoes.

33. ARTICHOKE & SPINACH DIP PIZZA

INGREDIENTS

1 prebaked 12-inch pizza crust

1 tablespoon of olive oil

1 cup of spinach dip

1 cup of shredded part-skim mozzarella cheese

1 jar (7-1/2 ounces) of marinated quartered artichoke hearts, drained

1/2 cup of oil-packed sun-dried tomatoes, patted dry and chopped

1/4 cup of chopped red onion

INSTRUCTIONS

Preheat your oven to 450 F.

Place crust on an ungreased pizza pan; brush with oil.

Spread spinach dip over top.

Sprinkle with cheese, artichokes, tomatoes and onion.

Bake until cheese is melted and edges are lightly browned, eight to ten minutes.

Cut into 24 pieces.

Enjoy!

34. REUBEN PIZZA

INGREDIENTS

A prebaked 12-inch pizza crust

2/3 cup of Thousand Island salad dressing

Half pound of sliced deli corned beef, cut into strips

1 can (14 ounces) of sauerkraut, rinsed and well drained

2 cups of shredded fine Swiss cheese

INSTRUCTIONS

Preheat oven to 400 F.

Place crust on an ungreased or parchment-lined baking sheet.

Spread with salad dressing.

Top with corned beef, sauerkraut and cheese.

Bake until cheese is melted, twelve to fifteen minutes.

Serve and enjoy!

35. TURKEY GYRO PIZZA

INGREDIENTS

- 2 cups of biscuit/baking mix
- 6 of tablespoons cold water
- 1/4 teaspoon of dried oregano
- 1/4 cup of Greek vinaigrette
- 1/2 cup of pitted Greek olives, sliced
- 1/2 cup of thinly sliced roasted sweet red pepper
- 1 & 1/2 cups of shredded part-skim mozzarella cheese
- 1/2 cup of crumbled feta cheese
- 1/2 cup of chopped cucumber
- A small tomato, chopped
- *Additional Greek vinaigrette, optional*

INSTRUCTIONS

Preheat oven to 425 F.

In a small bowl, combine biscuit mix, water and oregano to form a soft dough.

Press dough to fit a greased 12-in. pizza pan; pinch edge to form a rim.

Bake ten to twelve minutes or until lightly browned.

Brush a 1/4 cup vinaigrette over crust; top with olives, red pepper and cheeses.

Bake eight to ten minutes or until cheese is melted and crust is lightly browned.

Sprinkle with cucumber and tomato before serving.

If desired, drizzle with additional vinaigrette.

36. CRANBERRY, BRIE & TURKEY PIZZA

INGREDIENTS

- A prebaked 12-inch pizza crust
- 1 cup of whole-berry cranberry sauce
- 1 teaspoon of grated orange zest
- 2 cups of shredded part-skim mozzarella cheese
- 1 cup of coarsely shredded cooked turkey
- 1/2 of small red onion, thinly sliced
- 4 ounces of Brie cheese, cubed
- A tablespoon minced fresh rosemary

INSTRUCTIONS

Preheat oven to 450 F.

Place crust on an ungreased baking sheet.

In a small bowl, mix cranberry sauce and orange zest; spread over crust.

Top with mozzarella cheese, turkey, onion and Brie cheese; sprinkle with rosemary.

Bake ten to twelve minutes or until cheese is melted.

37. NEW HAVEN CLAM PIZZA

INGREDIENTS

- A package (1/4 ounce) active dry yeast
- 1 cup of warm water (110 F to 115 F)
- 1 teaspoon of white sugar
- 2 & 1/2 cups all-purpose flour
- 1 teaspoon of salt
- 2 tablespoons of canola oil
- 2 cans (6 & 1/2 ounces each) of chopped clams, drained
- 4 bacon strips, cooked and crumbled
- 3 garlic cloves, minced
- 2 tablespoons of grated Parmesan cheese
- 1 teaspoon of dried oregano
- 1 cup of shredded mozzarella cheese

INSTRUCTIONS

In a large bowl, dissolve yeast in water.

Add sugar; let stand for five minutes.

Add the flour, salt and oil; beat until smooth.

Cover and let rise in a warm place until doubled, about 15-20 minutes.

Punch dough down.

Press onto the bottom and up the sides of a greased 14-in. pizza pan; build up edges slightly.

Prick dough several times with a fork.

Bake at 425° for six to eight minutes.

Sprinkle remaining ingredients over crust in order listed.

Bake for 13-15 minutes or until crust is golden and cheese is melted.

Cut into wedges.

38. SEAFOOD PIZZA

INGREDIENTS

- A pizza dough (store bought or self-made)
- 1 1/2 cups of peeled cooked shrimp
- 1 cup of crabmeat (can be fresh or imitation)
- 1 1/2 cups of shredded mozzarella cheese
- 1/4 cup of grated parmesan cheese (or Romano cheese)
- 3 -4 cloves of minced garlic
- 1 teaspoon of minced parsley
- Olive oil

INSTRUCTIONS

Sauté garlic in olive oil for several minutes.

Add shrimp and crabmeat, mixing well with garlic and olive oil.

Add parsley.

Sprinkle a half cup mozzarella on pizza crust.

Place crab/shrimp mixture on crust.

Cover with remaining cheeses.

Bake according to your pizza crust directions (typically, bake pizza until crust is golden brown and cheese is melted and bubbling, about fifteen minutes).

Cut and serve with cocktail sauce.

39. GREEK SALAD PIZZA

INGREDIENTS

- 1 teaspoon of olive oil, plus more for coating grill
- 4 pita rounds
- 1 & 1/4 cups of diagonally sliced Persian cucumber (about three cucumbers)
- 3/4 cup of halved cherry tomatoes
- 1/2 cup of halved Greek Kalamata olives
- 2 ounces of crumbled Greek feta cheese (about 1/2 cup)
- 1/4 cup of thinly sliced red onion
- 1/4 teaspoon of kosher salt
- 1/2 cup of hummus

INSTRUCTIONS

Preheat your oven to 450 F.

Lightly coat a grill pan with oil; heat over medium-high.

Place pita rounds, two at a time, on grill pan; cook, turning once, until warm, about three minutes.

Toss together cucumber, tomatoes, olives, Greek feta, onion, and salt in a medium bowl.

Spread two tablespoons hummus on each pita round; top each with ¾ cup cucumber salad.

40. LEMON & SMOKED MOZZARELLA PIZZA

INGREDIENTS

- 1 lb. of prepared pizza dough
- 1/2 lb. of smoked mozzarella
- 1 small lemon
- 1 & 1/2 tbsp. of olive oil
- 1/2 tsp. of kosher salt
- 1/4 tsp. of ground black pepper

INSTRUCTIONS

Preheat oven to 450 degrees F.

Stretch and press dough with your fingers into a 14-inch circle on a large pizza pan or stone.

Arrange mozzarella and lemon slices over the crust, drizzle with oil, and sprinkle with salt and pepper.

Bake until golden brown and bubbly, about twenty minutes.

Cut into slices and serve immediately.

APPENDIX

In this section, you can find some basic pizza dough recipes for your convenience. Enjoy!

BASIC PIZZA DOUGH 1

INGREDIENTS

- 440ml of warm water
- 40g package of active dry yeast
- 2 tsps of salt
- 360-380g of strong flour
- 3 tbsps of olive oil, plus more for bowl
- Cornmeal, for pan

INSTRUCTIONS

Preheat oven at 220C/Gas 8.

Measure out 440ml warm water (it should be pleasantly warm on your wrist). Sprinkle the yeast on top of the water and allow it to activate, about 10 minutes.

Put the salt and 280g of the flour into a food processor. Pulse five times to blend. Pour in the yeast and water and pulse five more times.

Add the olive oil. Add the remaining flour, 1 cup at a time, pulsing and scraping the sides of the bowl until well blended.

As soon as the mixture is combined, dump it out onto a well-floured board and knead for 15 turns. The dough will become smooth and elastic-like.

Place the dough in a greased bowl and turn to coat all sides. Cover with clingfilm or a tea towel. Allow the dough to rise in a warm place for 45 minutes, until doubled in size, and then punch it down.

Divide dough in half; each half will make one pizza. You can make two pizzas or freeze half the dough for another time. Freeze the dough in a resealable freezer bag.

To thaw, remove the bag from the freezer and place in the refrigerator for 24 hours. Roll the dough out while cold and then allow it to come to room temperature before adding toppings.

BASIC PIZZA DOUGH 2

INGREDIENTS

- 2 to 2 1/3 cups of all-purpose flour OR bread flour[1] divided (250-295g)
- A packet of instant yeast (2 1/4 teaspoon)
- 1 1/2 teaspoons of sugar
- 3/4 teaspoon of salt
- 1/8-1/4 teaspoon of garlic powder and/or dried basil leaves optional
- 2 Tablespoons of olive oil
- 3/4 cup of warm water (175ml)

INSTRUCTIONS

Combine 1 cup (125g) of flour, instant yeast, sugar, and salt in a large bowl. If desired, add garlic powder and dried basil at this point as well.

Add olive oil and warm water and use a wooden spoon to stir well very well.

Gradually add another 1 cup (125g) of flour. Add any additional flour as needed (We've found that sometimes I need as much as an additional 1/3 cup), stirring until the dough is forming into a cohesive, elastic ball and is beginning to pull away from the sides of the bowl.

The dough will still be slightly sticky but still should be manageable with your hands.

Drizzle a separate, large, clean bowl generously with olive oil and use a pastry brush to brush up the sides of the bowl.

Lightly dust your hands with flour and form your pizza dough into a round ball and transfer to your olive oil-brushed bowl.

Use your hands to roll the pizza dough along the inside of the bowl until it is coated in olive oil, then cover the bowl tightly with plastic wrap and place it in a warm place.

Allow dough to rise for 30 minutes or until doubled in size.

If you intend to bake this dough into a pizza, we also recommend preheating your oven to 425F (215C) at this point so that it will have reached temperature once your pizza is ready to bake.

Once the dough has risen, use your hands to gently deflate it and transfer to a lightly floured surface and knead briefly until smooth (about three to five times).

Use either your hands or a rolling pin to work the dough into 12" circle.

Transfer dough to a parchment paper lined pizza pan and either pinch the edges or fold them over to form a crust.

Drizzle additional olive oil (about a tablespoon) over the top of the pizza and use your pastry brush to brush the entire surface of the pizza (including the crust) with olive oil.

Use a fork to poke holes all over the center of the pizza to keep the dough from bubbling up in the oven.

Add desired toppings and bake in a 425 F (215 C) preheated oven for 13-15 minutes or until toppings are golden brown. Slice and serve.

BASIC PIZZA DOUGH 3

INGREDIENTS

- 2 envelopes (1/4 ounce each) of active dry yeast (not rapid-rise)
- 2 tablespoons of sugar
- 1/4 cup of extra-virgin olive oil, plus more for bowl and brushing
- 2 teaspoons of kosher salt
- 4 cups of unbleached all-purpose flour (spooned and leveled), plus more for dusting

---

INSTRUCTIONS

Pour 1 1/2 cups warm water into a large bowl; sprinkle with yeast and let stand until foamy, about 5 minutes.

Whisk sugar, oil, and salt into yeast mixture.

Add flour and stir until a sticky dough forms. Transfer dough to an oiled bowl and brush top with oil.

Cover bowl with plastic wrap and set aside in a warm, draft-free place until dough has doubled in bulk, about an hour.

Turn out onto a lightly floured surface and gently knead 1 or 2 times before using.

Dough can be stored in an oiled bowl, covered with plastic, in refrigerator up to two hours.

To freeze, wrap dough in plastic and freeze in a resealable freezer bag up to three months.

If you plan to use it in a recipe that calls for half a batch, divide it before freezing.

Printed in Great Britain
by Amazon

62729782R00031